HOW NEARLY ANYONE CAN START A MICROCHURCH

Plant a Church Without Leaving Your Job

RALPH MOORE

EXPONENTIAL

How Nearly Anyone Can Start a Microchurch: Plant a Church Without Leaving Your Job
Copyright © 2021 by Ralph Moore

Exponential is a growing movement of activists committed to the multiplication of healthy new churches. Exponential Resources spotlights actionable principles, ideas and solutions for the accelerated multiplication of healthy, reproducing faith communities. For more information, visit exponential.org.

All rights reserved. No part of this book, including icons and images, may be reproduced in any manner without prior written permission from copyright holder, except where noted in the text and in the case of brief quotations embodied in critical articles and reviews.

Any internet addresses (websites, blogs, etc.) in this book are offered as a resource. They are not intended in any way to be or imply an endorsement by Exponential; nor does Exponential vouch for the content of these sites and contact numbers for the life of this book.

Scriptures marked ESV are taken from The Holy Bible, English Standard Version® (ESV®) Copyright © 2001 by Crossway, a publishing ministry of Good News Publishers. All rights reserved.

Scripture quotations marked MSG are taken from The Message, Copyright © 1993, 2002, 2018 by Eugene H. Peterson. Used by permission of NavPress. All rights reserved. Represented by Tyndale House Publishers, a Division of Tyndale House Ministries.

Scripture quotations marked NIV are taken from the Holy Bible, New International Version®, NIV®. Copyright © 1973, 1978, 1984, 2011 by Biblica, Inc.® Used by permission of Zondervan. All rights reserved worldwide. www.zondervan.com. The "NIV" and "New International Version" are trademarks registered in the United States Patent and Trademark Office by Biblica, Inc.®

Scripture quotations marked NKJV are taken from the New King James Version®. Copyright © 1982 by Thomas Nelson. Used by permission. All rights reserved.

Scripture quotations marked NLT are taken from the Holy Bible, New Living Translation. Copyright © 1996, 2004, 2015 by Tyndale House Foundation. Used by permission of Tyndale House Ministries, Carol Stream, Illinois 60188. All rights reserved.

Scripture quotations marked TLB are taken from The Living Bible, copyright © 1971 by Tyndale House Foundation. Used by permission of Tyndale House Publishers, Carol Stream, Illinois 60188. All rights reserved.

Italics have been added to Scripture quotations by the author.

ISBN: 978-1-62424-075-1 (paperback)
ISBN: 978-1-62424-076-8 (epub)

Content Director: Patt Alderdice Senseman
Interior Design: Karis Pratt
Editor: Karen Cain
Cover Design: Matt Wish

Printed in the United States of America.

ACKNOWLEDGEMENTS

I want to thank Todd Wilson for introducing me to the concept of planting microchurches. Todd's effort to return the American church to making disciples and multiplying churches gave new meaning to my life experience. I also thank Brian Sanders, who has led the way for so many of us. Brian's example in the Tampa Underground opened new vistas for me and many others.

Had I known these men when we planted the first Hope Chapel, I believe we could have produced many more congregations at a much-reduced cost to the sending church and with less risk to those we commissioned.

INSIDE

Introduction: Why You Should Read This Book	1
Chapter 1: Old but Still Learning	3
Chapter 2: The First Church Ever!	10
Chapter 3: What Is a Microchurch?	19
Chapter 4: Why Start Microchurches?	28
Chapter 5: Who Should Start a Microchurch (or Several)?	36
Chapter 6: How to Start a Microchurch	47
Chapter 7: A Template to Modify (Plus a Few Tips)	53
Appendix A: Questions to Loosen Up a New Group	63
Appendix B: Suggested Scriptures for Discussion	65
A Note from Ralph	67
Endnotes	69
About the Author	71

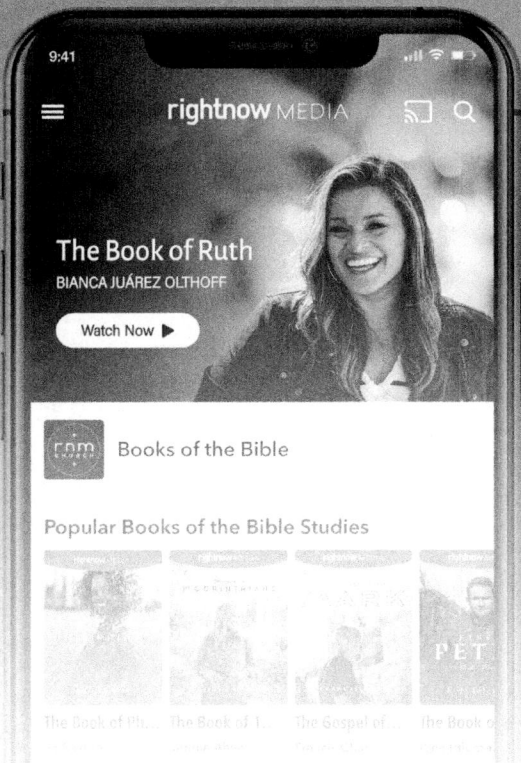

INTRODUCTION
Why You Should Read This Book

Are you hungry for more of Jesus? For more ministry? Deeper relationships? A better shot at evangelism?

If you check any of those boxes, this book is for you. You may be a pastor hoping to expand your reach or a church member looking to make a more significant impact. Perhaps you're young and frustrated with church as you find it.

I think you'll find answers in these few pages to whatever itch you're trying to scratch.

- Perhaps you feel disenfranchised by leaders who don't recognize your gifts.
- Maybe the church you lead doesn't do enough to serve underprivileged people.
- Maybe you have evangelized and discipled a workplace acquaintance but feel that person wouldn't fit in at a prevailing-model church.
- Perhaps you were called to lead a church but didn't, for whatever reason.

- Maybe you invested in a seminary education only to discover that you weren't cut out to lead a congregation in the prevailing church model.

But change is in the air. The COVID-19 pandemic drew many church volunteers deeper into ministry. People got used to more intimacy in smaller groups, etc.

Parking lot attendants and ushers suddenly led small gatherings of believers in Zoom meetings or Facebook groups. These people got a taste for congregational leadership and now feel capable of greater ministry.

Sensing the Spirit working through you in the life of another person is addictive. Did you ever know someone addicted to crack cocaine? One hit off the pipe, and a person will do just about anything to get back to it.

Similarly, one profound ministry moment triggers a *healthy* addiction. But our churches aren't leading people to minister to friends—sometimes they're not even helping people explore Spirit-driven encounters with God.

We teach people *about* God then teach them to *operate programs*. However, our structures don't much allow for interfacing with him.

In the following few pages, I'll share three simple questions that you can use to help friends encounter God. The questions will also help you lead small groups, which we'll call *microchurches*.

Whatever the issue you find yourself facing, one solution may be to plant a microchurch. You can keep your job, remain in your home church, and still reach a small congregation of people who might not otherwise come to know God.

So, grab a cup of coffee, and let's get into this.

CHAPTER 1

Old but Still Learning

I planted a microchurch during the pandemic lockdown.

It wasn't my first, but it was my first autonomous and intentionally small group. We're a digital church who meets via Zoom for two increasingly intimate hours every Saturday. And we recently assumed leadership of a second microchurch in San Diego, where I live.

Our members live in Texas, Tennessee, Arizona, and in four California cities. We came out of the gate a little awkward and uncomfortable, but gradually we settled in, becoming more open and intimate. Now we laugh, enjoy encouraging fellowship, share God's Word, and even sing together (badly). It's fun!

A Model That Served Us Well

I've helped plant mostly mid-sized churches throughout my adult life. Two that my wife and I planted grew to a little more than 2,000 in attendance, and the third, which we planted in our late sixties, topped out at around 300 people. Together we managed to launch eight churches in our six-year tenure. So, I knew a decent amount about church multiplication but precious little about planting microchurches—free-standing microchurches, that is.

Although this is my first shot at leading an autonomous microchurch, I've started and led dozens. The difference is that, until now, they were inside the circle of our congregation. Think of the old cell-church model, and you'll have a pretty good grasp of what we were about. Our team would start a microchurch, disciple apprentice leaders, leave the established group under the care of the strongest apprentice, and then plant another. Rinse and repeat, as often as practical.

If one of those apprentices replicated the process three times, we began looking at that person as a potential church planter—again shooting for a mid-size launch.

Adding a New Approach

In those days, church planters would often leave their employment to go full-time with a church. That approach now seems impractical, given the spiritual and material climate.

Real estate costs are out of control. The ever more-divided population of our country grows more hostile to the Church. City governments don't want churches because they remove properties from the tax rolls. The world has changed a great deal from what I enjoyed as a church multiplier less than a decade ago.

Things are challenging but not impossible. Jesus is still Lord, and his Church will prevail—but it will do so differently. We will come through these times looking more like the church he planted in Jerusalem than those getting off the ground in America's past few decades. And that's a good thing!

That's not to say that the model that served us so well will disappear. We need that approach, among many others! But if we hope to engage the nooks and crannies of society, we need a smaller vehicle—one capable of penetrating those cracks to engage the spiritual needs of people who find themselves lost in a fog without Jesus. Evangelism increasingly happens outside of church buildings. It's a friendship-based endeavor. Social media opens many doors but leaves people hungry for face-to-face intimacy, which occurs in smaller groups better than crowds. The future, as always, will differ from the past.

A New Kind of Leader

We're looking for mature believers who can maintain a job or career while planting a microchurch in a home, park, coffee shop, food court, conference room, or even in a service bay at an auto repair shop.

None of this is very different from what Rick Warren did in the living room of his apartment several decades ago. The significant differences between what we're seeing now and what Rick did then were his seminary education and a heavy dose of outside funding.

But we've discovered that disciplemaking in a local church is a more-than-adequate education for a church planter. And there's no arguing that a person with a job or career brings huge financial capital to a church plant. Taking a cue from Rick, a microchurch needn't remain micro. It can grow to any size, and a pastor may end up on a church payroll. That is all wonderful, but it is no longer the ideal starting place.

The best starting point is a microchurch led by a freelance pastor who is discipled in a church and who then starts a new congregation with little financial overhead.

Why This Book?

A few years ago, my friend Todd Wilson presented an 11-page paper on microchurches to about 30 of our peers during a lunch break at the Orlando Exponential conference. It was well-received, but toward the end of the meeting, one leader surfaced several questions that neither Todd nor the rest of us anticipated. We were left realizing that we needed better answers to the questions "What is a church?" and "What is a disciple?"

The upshot was that Todd asked me to write a book that would give us a bigger target for bouncing off our thoughts and insights. That book (available at Exponential.org) is called *Mega Multi Micro*. The foundational concepts include that: a) megachurches grew while the Church shrank for five decades; b) multi-sites helped growing congregations solve real-estate problems, but we still shrank; and c) times have changed, and we need to think "micro" to redeem our place in the larger culture.

When I wrote that book, I'd only planted microchurches within the circle of the congregations I'd led. We called them "minichurches." We began this in the 1970s, an era of miniskirts, minicars, and—minichurches. However, the term was *not* frivolous or without purpose. We wanted people to see that the "mini" version was as much a real church as a few thousand people gathered on the weekend.

As I began writing, I immediately encountered a problem. I could find only seven or eight examples of what would qualify as an autonomous microchurch in our Hope Chapel family. So, being a reasonably astute person, I told all seven or eight stories. But I still didn't know much about launching (from a larger congregation) or independently planting autonomous microchurches.

Write a book, they say, and you'll become an expert! That truism works for some. For me, it was neither true nor funny.

Once the book came out, I soon found myself being interviewed in webinars and podcasts. Todd's original concept hit a live nerve, and people were hungry for something that smacked of a New Testament archetype. Teaching about this was not always fun. I felt like a fraud, answering questions while trying to wed my scant knowledge of the micro with a strong dose of mid-size church multiplication experience.

Relief came in the form of my podcast. It launched as a teaching series based loosely on the *MMM* book, but it soon became something different. I chose to interview leaders of small-to-mid-size congregations bent on launching microchurch networks. And I'm still learning from the podcast guests as I go!

Occasionally I get to interview people like those I'll feature in a later chapter, who successfully planted and are now reproducing microchurches. You see, I am old, but I'm still learning.

My purpose for this short book is to pass along some of what I've learned. It is the same reason I put three days each week into the content you find on RalphMoore.net. Technically retired, I try to fulfill my calling as a missionary to younger leaders. I believe these times call for us all to pool whatever we know of Jesus and his mission so we can best fulfill our small chunk of it.

Becoming a Level 5 Multiplying Church

You're likely reading this because you want to see the gospel reach your particular Jerusalem or Judea and spread to the ends of the earth. We've discovered that the best way to evangelize any population is by planting new churches. If every church reproduced itself in a similarly replicating congregation, we could quickly evangelize the world.

But few churches *do* reproduce. A decade ago, just 4% of U.S. churches had ever reproduced, including churches that reproduced by splitting. However, the efforts of Exponential.org and similar organizations have since borne fruit. By 2020, more than 7% of

American congregations had reproduced at least once. Sociologists say that 16% is the magic number where behavior becomes a norm for any society or culture. If we can get 16% of churches reproducing, we'll be off to the races!

But the real gold is not in simple reproduction (adding more congregations) but in multiplication, where the churches we launch can in turn launch churches without asking permission of the parent church. Adding "sites" or extension services is neither reproduction nor multiplication. It is a practical method for growing a single congregation, but it remains at what we call "Level 3 addition." Perhaps it's "Level 3.5," but it is not Level 4.

Let me explain the five levels of church effectiveness presented by my friends at Exponential.

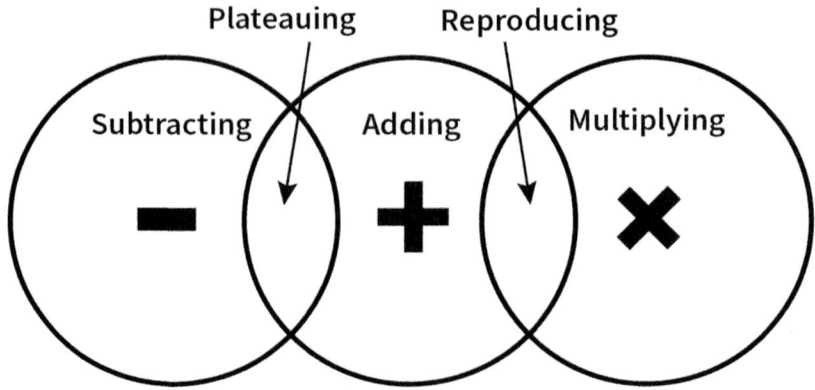

Source: *New to Five: Starting a Level 5 Multiplying Church* by Ralph Moore and Jeff Christopherson (Exponential, 2017).

Every church is either: a) subtracting (shrinking); b) plateauing (static); c) adding members; d) reproducing itself; or e) multiplying by planting new, autonomous churches without permission from the parent group.

A Level 5 multiplying church steps beyond closely held reproduction (Level 4) into planting autonomous churches, each of which is free to multiply others. Of course, multiplication is the goal—but that can be elusive if your church is small. The good news is that microchurches planted by freelance pastors open new doors to even the smallest congregations.

We're simply catching up to the rest of the world and history in many ways. Disciplemaking and church planting, as presented in Acts, are the archetype or benchmark for healthy reproduction. Wherever we find explosive church growth, we discover microchurch movements led by bivocational or freelance pastors.

CHAPTER 2

The First Church Ever!

Acts 1 and 2 describe a fantastic event.

After Jesus' death and resurrection, 120 believers assembled as the church at Jerusalem. An outstanding miracle caused them to add 3,000 members in a single day! I've always wondered what life was like the day following that growth explosion—and a week after that. Leaders must have found life both joyous and stressful at once.

Growth Is Nice, but Extreme Growth Is Confounding

Acts 2 says the believers met in the Jewish temple court, which held about 400 people (a far cry from 3,120). They also met in homes. The problem is that a Hebrew home maxed out at around 10 people. So where did they find leaders for 312 microchurches *in a single day?* Or many more than that just a few days later?

The juxtaposition between the large and small groups is worth noting, as it points us toward the solution. Microchurch networks benefit from gathering in larger groups from time to time. In addition to expanded fellowship, the larger gathering can keep everyone focused through in-depth teaching. The bigger meetings also afford a sense of momentum. But most God-encounters occur in smaller groups, where trust rides waves of intimacy.

The home groups in Acts weren't miniature knockoffs of the temple meetings. The leaders were new to following Christ, but since their principal activity was rehearsing the "apostles' teaching," they were mostly up to the task. There were only 12 apostles, so we know that they couldn't have made the rounds to hundreds of home churches. The model had to work around a discussion of what the leaders heard earlier, or it wouldn't have worked at all.

Remember, these Christians weren't carrying Bibles—they didn't have them. Their numbers quickly swelled to more than 5,000 men plus women and children (Acts 4:4), which means that they weren't all able to fit into the temple, even in large blocks spread over a week. Theirs was a house-church movement. As such, they paid no rent and probably didn't carry financial overhead in the form of salaries.

A Universal Biblical Model for a Church Meeting

In Acts 2:41-47, we read that the early Church functioned in the

- **Teaching (reflected)**
- **Fellowship**
- **Prayer**
- **Shared Meals**
- **Holy Communion**
- **Miracles/Praise**
- **Generosity**

Favor with Neighbors

Numbers Grew Daily

apostles' teaching, fellowship, prayer, shared meals, holy communion, miracles coupled with praise, and generosity. If you want to launch a microchurch, I suggest reading this passage every day for a month. You'll want to hit on all those elements, though perhaps not in every meeting.

Teaching

If you believe that God is real and Jesus is not a liar, then you believe his words, "But the Advocate, the Holy Spirit, whom the Father will send in my name, will teach you all things and will remind you of everything I have said to you" (John 14:26-27 NIV). A Spirit-driven leader will find the necessary guidance to lead a microchurch to great fruitfulness.

The earliest Christ-followers would have had the Old Testament coupled with the words of Jesus and whatever the apostles taught in the temple. After that, they had to learn together through discussion and interaction. We've elevated preachers to our detriment. A microchurch is a perfect format for Holy Spirit-led self-discovery of spiritual truth. Read and discuss Scripture, as I described earlier, and avoid preachiness and religious legalism, or you will fail.

Fellowship

We've discussed the need for intimacy. I have more "friends" than ever before because of Facebook. Many are old friends who I once knew quite well. Our relationships slowly drifted into acquaintanceships after losing touch due to busy schedules or living far apart. Others have read my books or heard me preach. They may be Facebook friends, but we share no actual face-to-face contact.

Because we live in a hurried world and do so much online, we interact less with real people. When I was five years old, my parents would have dinner with the folks who owned the corner grocery.

That sort of neighborliness dried up when I was in high school. Today, I will buy from Amazon rather than drive a half-mile to a store where I might learn a clerk's name. We even buy our groceries via home delivery!

Now, more than ever, people long for deep fellowship—and you can provide it if you plant a microchurch! Set aside plenty of time for friendship, and if someone is hurting, dump the scheduled discussion so you can focus everyone's attention on the wounded individual.

Prayer

The Bible teaches us to "share each other's troubles and problems, and so obey our Lord's command. If anyone thinks he is too great to stoop to this, he is fooling himself. He is really a nobody" (Galatians 6:2-3 TLB).

When we share another person's problems, prayer becomes prominent. I'm speaking of personalized prayer born of human need. It can only happen when one person bares their soul to another individual or to a group of trusted friends.

Make time for prayer, but don't get caught up praying for all the world's problems. Pray mainly for the people in the room and the things that concern them. The teaching, discussion, and fellowship should reveal the true prayer needs in your microchurch.

I've found that taking "prayer requests" works against praying for whatever surfaced during heartfelt conversation. I only want to focus prayer on issues that were important enough to come up in ordinary exchanges.

Shared Meals

Bring leftovers. Don't let your meetings turn into a baking contest. Inviting everyone to participate by bringing food helps equalize the load while instigating generosity. Everyone gives and receives. Jesus asked the woman at the well to provide him with water before he gave her Living Water. Bringing food makes for better fellowship while cultivating a culture of sharing.

Holy Communion

In Catholic and some European Protestant circles, believers share holy communion every time they meet. Many American Protestant churches do this monthly. There is no discernible pattern for this in Scripture. Jesus said to remember his suffering on our behalf whenever we shared holy communion. Paul later wrote, "For every time you eat this bread and drink this cup, you are retelling the message of the Lord's death, that he has died for you. Do this until he comes again" (1 Corinthians 11:26 TLB). In the broader context (26-33), Paul warned that participating in communion while not caring for others would result in God's anger.

So the only advice about communion in Scripture is to remember Jesus and to love each other, which may cost you time, energy, and even money.

Miracles/Praise

Most Christians sing hymns and Scripture songs in church. But, in an attempt at relevancy, some church services resemble rock concerts or Las Vegas acts. That physically can't happen in a microchurch.

Instead, we should praise God by thanking him for answers to prayer. One good thing about consistently spending time around food and in friendship is that people naturally inquire, "Hey, I prayed for you; what happened?" Praying and watching for God to act are keys to healthy growth and even conversion of the skeptical.

Generosity

Giving brings with it a problem unique to America. Our tax laws allow us to deduct charitable donations, including those made to churches. Tax deductions and financial records get sticky for microchurches for two reasons: a) there are few financial needs; and b) forming a government-compliant, nonprofit corporation for a dozen people is cumbersome at best.

The last church I planted launched a microchurch in Las Vegas, sending them off with a couple thousand dollars to hire an attorney and "get legal." The microchurch kept the money for a year and then returned it. The leader said it was too complicated for their small group to keep up with the government reports. He was right, but we didn't know how to overcome the problem!

After the leader returned the money, he and I went on a reading binge to discover what others were doing. We found that the best options were microchurch networks that gathered under a single nonprofit entity or those that remained connected to a "mother church." There was nothing to satisfy the free-standing microchurch.

Then I ran into an old friend, Wayne Ching.

Wayne is an engineer who has led a microchurch for nearly two decades. Theirs is a large group, numbering nearly 30 people. He told me they simply forego the tax deduction. They teach tithing (the practice of giving 10% of your income to God), but they do it a little differently than most churches.

Each member opens a checking account in his or her own name but with actual ownership assigned to Jesus (they don't inform the bank of this). Members deposit 10% of their income into these "tithing accounts" while retaining complete control over the money. They then give it away as they feel God leads them.

They might help a neighbor with rent or donate to help others in the aftermath of a hurricane. Some support an abused women's shelter, while others donate money to missionaries or to agencies rescuing people from the slave trade.

Wayne told me that he funds the financial overhead of their microchurch out of his personal tithe—mostly amounting to paper cups, coffee, books, and Bibles. He gives the rest to missionaries. This plan may not work for everyone, but it works well if you don't mind forgoing the tax deduction. (Almost 70% of people take the standard deduction and don't itemize for donations anyway.)

Reaching the Neighbors

In the last few words of Acts 2, we read, "The whole city was favorable to them, and each day God added to them all who were being saved" (Acts 2:47 TLB).

This activity was normative even before the religious authorities felt threatened by their growth and began persecuting these people. The upshot is that they did what Jesus asked. There are three great commandments in Jesus' teaching:

- "Love the Lord your God with all your heart and with all your soul and with all your mind and with all your strength" (Mark 12:30 NIV).
- "'Love your neighbor as yourself.' There is no commandment greater than these" (Mark 12:31 NIV).

- "Go and make disciples of all the nations, baptizing them in the name of the Father and the Son and the Holy Spirit. Teach these new disciples to obey all the commands I have given you. And be sure of this: I am with you always, even to the end of the age" (Matthew 28:19-20 NLT).

Jesus didn't say to build big churches or even to make converts. He told us to love God, love our neighbor (who may see the world very differently than we do), and to make disciples of those who don't yet know him.

The term *nations* comes from the original Greek text, *ethne*. It encompasses more than DNA and would be better understood as "people groups." People groups might include investment bankers in Shanghai or skateboarders in Santa Cruz. Iraqis whose families immigrated after the first Gulf War are the predominant people group in my neighborhood. Some tattoo parlors draw such a loyal crowd that they resemble small churches operating without Jesus—they may even have a leader who functions almost like a pastor.

Jesus left instructions to infiltrate every such group with the gospel. And the best example of how to do it seems to be that of the earliest Christ-followers. If we spend time loving our neighbors, Jesus will find ways to build his Church.

We still tend to mess up these three simple instructions. We love things more than God. We dislike people with whom we disagree. And we train converts in Bible doctrine rather than leading them into a Spirit-driven relationship with Jesus by discipling them to follow us as we follow Jesus. A headful of knowledge doesn't lead a person to become a disciple of Christ. Following a friend into that relationship does.

Disciplemaking vs. Discipleship

It seems that Jesus was talking about making friends with the neighbors and then introducing them to the God who loves them. Disciplemaking is bringing people *into* Christ and then helping them move to maturity in his love. This process explains why microchurches are such vital tools for changing our world.

The term *disciple* suggests that as one person learns from another, he or she becomes a disciple. Jesus called a group of men to "Follow Me, and I will make you fishers of men" (Matthew 4:19 NKJV). Paul invited, "Follow my example, as I follow the example of Christ" (1 Corinthians 11:1, NIV).

We need to rediscover the idea of discipling people *into* Christ rather than educating them *after* committing to Christ. To do this, you'll need to spend time with others—enough time for them to be interested in following you into that most important relationship with the Creator and his Son.

CHAPTER 3

What Is a Microchurch?

We toss around many different terms for what one could most easily describe as a "house church" that might, or might not, meet in a home or apartment. Because microchurches meet everywhere, from parks to corporate boardrooms to automotive garages, Christian leaders and authors struggle to find a label everyone understands. Terms like *simple church*, *café church*, *organic church*, *essential church*, and *New Testament church* are all attempts to simply define a small group of believers gathering around the activities we discover in Acts 2:41-47.

The term *microchurch* is not new, but it is gaining traction. That is why I use it in this book.

Today about six million Americans meet in microchurches.[1] Microchurches involve one-fifth as many Americans as attend megachurches. But you can bet that microchurch members know each other intimately, as relationships decrease when church size increases.

My friend Dave Ferguson reminds us, "Those who own the language own the paradigm. Those who own the paradigm own the future." For too long, the language and paradigm have been in the hands of scholars rather than movement makers. And, since most movements begin at the grassroots level, people like you and me need to busy ourselves with defining language and organizing a paradigm for the future.

Function and Form

I like to think in terms of function and form.

I think that four great functions describe the Church: a) teaching God's Word (mostly taught rather than organized into clever sermons); b) fellowship (real community); c) worship in the Romans 12 sense of living surrender; and d) mission, as we reach outside ourselves and our circle to bless others. You can observe these four functions in Acts 2:41-47.

As to form, Jesus promised to be present whenever two or more of us gather in his name. So a few people meeting together in a home in Jerusalem the day after Pentecost would qualify as a church. Let's assume that any gathering of Christ-followers (form) that meets the criteria of the four functions *is* a church. You can ask of any such group, "Is this truly a church?" By that standard, many larger congregations would fail to meet the conditions and should not be called churches.

I've been in megachurches where little community or fellowship was possible. I've led microchurches that lacked mission. You get the picture. Churches are not defined by elder boards, a pastor's education, or congregation size but by Christ-serving people on a mission who are learning to be the Church in whatever circumstances they happen to encounter.

Synagogue as Microchurch

In Acts 12, we observe a prayer meeting in a home while Peter was in prison. We've mentioned several other instances of people hosting churches in their homes. But to fully grasp the idea of churches in homes, we need to understand synagogue worship during New Testament times, as the synagogue influenced the house churches.

The word *synagogue* literally means "gathering." The Gospels describe Jesus attending and preaching in synagogues. Paul usually preached to Jews in a synagogue before addressing the non-Jewish community.

Synagogues trace their history to the destruction of Jerusalem by Nebuchadnezzar around 597 BC.[2] They became an Old Testament version of what we're now calling a microchurch.

While the Jews were in exile under Persian King Cyrus, all worship centered around the synagogue or gathering. Since these people were captives and enslaved people, it was only natural that they met in homes—they hadn't the resources to construct purpose-built structures. Upon their return to Jerusalem under Ezra and Nehemiah, in 539 BC, they re-established temple worship. But the synagogue remained a part of Jewish life. It was the model for the earliest churches.

What happened after Jesus met the woman at the well in Samaria (John 4)? The entire village professed belief that he was the Messiah. Do you think they didn't gather to seek God once Jesus left town? What about the other places where Jesus taught and performed miracles? They would either have converted the synagogue or set up a parallel system. I'd call their gatherings churches.

The Power of Multiplication

I've often been challenged with the question, "Is planting microchurches all you do?" The answer is "No." One of the churches in our network numbers more than 10,000 people. Another more than 5,000. Several others are larger than 1,000. But the power is in multiplication.

If we start 100 microchurches, some will grow large while others multiply. The sweet spot is when they do both. Either additional growth or multiplication will produce fruit, but multiplication boasts possibilities lacking in simple church-growth addition.

We started a microchurch with just 12 people in an empty church building. It grew into a movement of 2,600+ "macrochurches." Those congregations encompass nearly a quarter-million people. That's good, but the model requires very gifted people and many financial resources.

Imagine a movement of a thousand 30-member microchurches. It would include 30,000 people and could be developed at nearly zero financial cost, as church planters would be trained in local churches and they, in turn, would equip others.

If maintaining a career while serving as a freelance pastor became normative in the United States, we could generate leadership much faster than we did during my tenure as a church multiplier. Granted, people are busier than ever, but leading a tiny church while holding a job or career makes delegation easier than when the congregation pays you. Besides, in a better-connected group, people tend to buy in by stepping up their involvement and willingness to serve each other. (The bonus here is that many of those reached may be people who either avoid your standard church or feel marginalized by it.)

Countering conventional "churchthink" opens new vistas for the Western church. And if we made it to more than 2,600 churches while carrying a heavy financial burden, the thought of a thousand microchurches suddenly feels like a very low estimate of what the Spirit could do through people like you.

What It Is Not

The concept of freelance-led microchurches is in danger of becoming the latest fad in the Christian church. Such trendiness is sad because it is the go-to model in most of the world. Think about believers operating in extreme poverty, under persecution, or amid Islamic culture. These folks can only plant and lead churches that look like what we see in Acts 2:41-47—a far cry from what we're used to seeing on the streets of America. But as the concept grows in popularity, we need to be clear that a micro-version of your typical prevailing-model Western church is *not* what we're attempting.

I recently heard a man talking about how he had assembled a core team and how they were busy building an online marketing plan for the upcoming launch of their microchurch. That may be OK, but it misses the point.

We need to reach unreached people groups by befriending someone who looks and acts like a Luke 10 "person of peace" (who probably doesn't yet know Christ). The power starts with one or two people who can reach others in their group and build out from there. Then you plan to leave the group in the hands of this person or another disciple as you head out to replicate the process. This progression is microchurch planting in action.

The Jesus Model

The New Testament reports numbers throughout the ministry of Jesus and into the early days of the church at Jerusalem. After that, Christianity turned into a motley movement, casting aside the issue of reporting numbers. But some numbers are crucial to disciple-making. These are 3, 12, and 120.

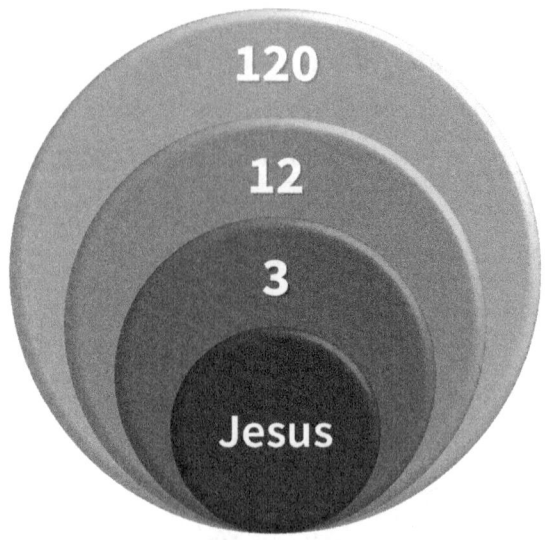

Perhaps the most important set of numbers in the Bible are 3, 12, and 120 as they present a template of Jesus' disciplemaking efforts and immediate results.

The 3

Jesus had an inner circle of three disciples: Peter, James, and John. These men got the most attention and emulated Jesus as teachers and healers after the resurrection. But the Bible never reports that they discipled anyone after the resurrection! They probably did, but the Bible never mentions it—standing sharply in contrast to Barnabas and Paul, as recorded in Acts.

For starters, Barnabas mentored and championed Saul of Tarsus. According to Luke in Acts, both Barnabas and Saul/Paul made disciples in small groups and individually. They imitated Jesus in that regard. We should do the same if we intend to spread biblical values to those around us. Preaching and teaching are fine, but close relationships among dedicated people can change the world.

The 12

I may be stretching this, but if Peter, James, and John each looked after three others, that would make up the whole company of Jesus' 12 disciples. I don't know that they did this, and they certainly never show any evidence of it after the resurrection, but it does seem plausible.

The primary lesson here is that people surrounded Jesus in concentric circles beginning with a close inner circle, then spreading to a slightly larger group of would-be leaders. Coincidentally, we've found that *just about anyone* can lead a microchurch of 12 people.

The 120

After the resurrection, the church in Jerusalem numbered 120 people. I constantly challenge the pastors of smaller churches to pray toward 120 rather than five or six thousand. It's frustrating to watch people laboring in small towns or lacking grand leadership skills grow depressed because they compare the size of their congregations to that of a megachurch pastor they heard at a conference.

If you decide to lead a microchurch, try to build a network that equals the size of the church that Jesus planted in Jerusalem. If your church grows larger than his, remember that "from everyone who has been given much, much will be demanded" (Luke 12:48 NIV). If your church is more prominent than what Jesus left after three years in and around Jerusalem, you surely need to multiply churches.

Everybody Plays

You know the old saw, "The NFL fields 22 men desperately needing rest in front of 70,000 others who desperately need exercise." It's memorable because it is true.

It's also descriptive of most churches. A few people do all the work (and hold the power, appointed or implicit) while the rest remain spectators. This ought not to be.

Scripture teaches us, "When you gather for worship, *each one of you* be prepared with something that will be useful for all: Sing a hymn, teach a lesson, tell a story, lead a prayer, provide an insight" (1 Corinthians 14:26 MSG).

In a healthy church, everybody plays.

We should "carry each other's burdens, and in this way, . . . fulfill the law of Christ" (Galatians 6:2 NIV). "Admit your faults to one another and pray for each other so that you may be healed" (James 5:16 TLB). "Let us think of ways to motivate one another to acts of love and good works. And let us not neglect our meeting together, as some people do, but encourage one another, especially now that the day of his return is drawing near" (Hebrews 10:24-25 NLT).

All these things work best in face-to-face circles, where intimate contact results in solid ministry.

It's Not Difficult!

Paul wrote the classic theology of Christianity as a letter to the church in Rome. When he wrote, he began by apologizing for not having visited there (Romans 1). Yet toward the end of the book, he penned three assumptions about people he had never met (he never met you either, but the assumptions are just as valid for you as for the Roman believers): "I myself am convinced, my brothers and sisters, that you yourselves are full of goodness, filled with knowledge and competent to instruct one another" (Romans 15:14 NIV).

The key to those three assumptions is found in the first, "You yourselves are full of goodness." None of us is good on our own. We will abuse our neighbors and resort to ultimate selfishness in times of difficulty. It is only through reconciliation with God that we gain the ability to overcome our self-centered tendencies and live for others. This goodness comes through the redemptive presence and empowerment of God's Spirit in us.

The Spirit's work is the key to the other two assumptions. Completeness in knowledge assumes the Spirit acts as a teacher, applying God's words to our hearts and minds (John 14:26). The ability to instruct one another also comes from the Spirit and his gifts. In short, if you are walking in a relationship with God, you can bless your brothers and sisters.

If you fit these standards, you—or anyone else—qualify to lead a church. Notice that there is no reference to professional theological training mentioned in this passage. Nor can you find it elsewhere in the New Testament. Instead, you'll see examples of people like Timothy and Titus, who were discipled into ministry by the people before them. As to the qualifications for leadership, the New Testament word pastor means one who "looks after a flock, not merely feeds them." If you plant a microchurch, you must disciple others to do the same. All of us who follow Christ are called to make disciples where we live, work, and play.

CHAPTER 4

Why Start Microchurches?

We're not fulfilling the Great Commission.

The number of Christ-followers in the West continues to shrink while growing in other places. Jesus told us to go *make disciples of all people* (Matthew 28:19). Instead, we stay where we are and build bigger congregations.

We're Shrinking

But we're not even good at that. American megachurches account for fewer than 10% of all churchgoers. Evangelical Christianity is losing its share of our population at a rate of around 1% per decade.

The evangelical segment of the U.S. population fell by 0.9% between 2007 and 2014.[3] And this was before COVID-19 further upset the apple cart. Some studies estimate that as many as 30% of pre-COVID church attenders did not, and will not, return.

Congregations are closing at a rapid clip post-COVID, but we were in trouble even before the pandemic. From 2000 to 2005, we needed an annual net gain of 3,205 new churches to keep up with population growth. We got 303. We fell short by more than 17,000 church plants in six years. That is a deficit of 2,902 new churches per year.[4] A recent survey suggests that 38% of pastors whose churches survived the COVID lockdown now consider leaving the ministry. We clearly need a different approach.

Starting a small church in a home, park, or coffee shop won't solve the problem—but if we start enough of them, we can turn the tide.

The Western World Is in a Post-Christian Mode

We face radical secularism from both the left and right ends of the political spectrum.

That's a bummer, but the good news is that our culture is *not* unlike that faced by the earliest believers. The Church grew from nothing to about 1.8 million people (out of 250 million people) by AD 200. And most of that growth took place in house churches or microchurches (small churches that met in homes, caves, or on riverbanks). God has walked this path before. We just need to realign ourselves to walk it with him.

Christianity currently grows faster in Nepal than anywhere else. Nearly all the growth is in microchurches. Nigeria boasts the highest rate of Christ-followers per capita. Again, microchurches led by discipleship-trained pastors are the rule, not the exception. Sadly, many of these pastors lead microchurches while seeking to copy America by growing megachurches—so, dashed expectations are pretty standard. Exported American ideas often outshine biblical standards.

Microchurches are simple and easy to lead. Traditional, prevailing-model churches are not. The larger the church, the more administrative skill, charisma, money, and programs necessary to attract and retain people. What attracts people is what they will continue to demand. The attractional, consumer-driven church is a monster that is hungry for more and more resources—if you build it, you must fuel it!

Microchurches, by contrast, require no contrived programs, little administrative skill, and a leader who is merely able to lead a discussion—not even preach a sermon. And the chances of people interactively engaging God in prayer, miracles, and changed lives are far more significant in face-to-face groups than in large spectator-oriented audiences. Again, if you build it, you must fuel it; but that's a lot easier at a micro rather than mega level.

Reasons to Plant a Microchurch

There are probably a dozen reasons for planting a microchurch. We'll look at a few of them here. But before you embark on any journey, you should be sure that you have a pure heart and know the *why* before attempting the *what*. Without an adequate why, you'll give up on the what at the first whiff of difficulty.

Reason 1: Return to New Testament Model

Several times the Bible depicts Christ-followers meeting in homes.

Aquila and Priscilla hosted a church in their home (1 Corinthians 16:19 and Romans 16:3-5). It appears that they did this in two different cities while supporting themselves as tentmakers (a choice, not a fallback).

Someone named Nympha hosted a church in her house in Laodicea (Colossians 4:15). And we read of believers meeting in homes from the very start (Acts 2:41-47).

Paul first engaged God-fearers worshipping by a river in Philippi. By the time he had evangelized them and done a stint in jail, he met with these newly minted believers in the home of their leader, a woman named Lydia (Acts 16:11-40).

After Roman Emperor Constantine legalized and politicized the Church (thus diluting its fervor), believers began spending money on church buildings, a stilted hierarchy, and expensive trappings, which cooled disciplemaking fervor and eventually led to the Dark Ages.

Reason 2: Money Matters

One motive for planting a microchurch is to release funds for actual ministry to people rather than investing it in buildings, salaries, and programs.

In 2001, the cost of baptizing an individual in the United States was $1.5 million (including buildings, programs, and salaries to get them there).[5] It costs less money per baptism overseas, but it's still outrageous. Gordon Conwell's Center for the Study of Global Christianity (CSGC) examined the global cost of baptizing one person in 2014; it came in at $753,000. Again, this would include the cost of everything from full-time missionaries to short-term mission teams. It involves salaries for indigenous leaders and the construction of churches and schools. But it is excessive. There is a better way.

Reason 3: Rejection

Sometimes an existing church changes course or moves away from its founding values or theology. At this point, a few members show their hesitation, arousing the leader's ire. These folks are often cast aside and left out. They may be asked to leave. More often, they get marginalized. Either way, they are rejected. When this happens, it is good to band together to *preserve* their friendship and identity as a group.

While this isn't the best reason to plant a microchurch, it is valid. One warning: you should never attempt to harm the church you leave behind if you do this.

Reason 4: Disappointment and Unfulfilled Calling

Some have left the pastorate because of their unmet personal expectations. Others got assigned to a church where they didn't match the congregation's expectations.

The prevailing model is for a young person to fulfill a call to ministry by graduating from a Bible college or seminary (often incurring massive debt) and then spend a lifetime leading a church that pays a full-time salary and returns love and fellowship to its leader.

But things don't always work this way. Pastors may discover that their gifts only match the needs of a smaller congregation. Limited abilities force them into secular jobs while being expected to carry a church workload like the leader down the road who is being paid for full-time commitment to a congregation. Others have met an intransient church board or some other influential group who opposes every move they make. Either way, disappointment drives thousands of pastors from active ministry every year.

The idea of building a meaningful and financially rewarding career outside the Church while planting and leading a microchurch is a way to fulfill those spiritual stirrings that led you toward pastoral leadership many years ago. And you may find that a new beginning at the micro level leads to something more significant. There is no law requiring a microchurch to remain "micro."

Reason 5: Spiritual Intimacy

We all crave intimacy: the larger the congregation, the more distant the relationships. The New Testament defines the Greek word *koinonia* as "partnership" or "community." In Acts 2, koinonia immediately follows the apostles' teaching in a prioritized list of activities.

It even precedes prayer—this makes sense, in that it is difficult to pray with passion for someone you don't know.

Younger people are leaving the Church because they disdain expensive programs while experiencing little intimacy. Some reject what they would call a "false gospel" of glamor and crowds while searching for something that soothes their souls.

The United States is a vast mission field, involving 584 "unreached and unengaged" people groups.[6] The standouts are among the Millennial generation. Think of them as a "Millennial mission field." Their numbers are greater than the population of many small countries. They seem uninterested in the gospel, or perhaps just uninterested in the Church as it presents itself in the United States. This digitally connected generation responds quite well to face-to-face churches in smaller settings.

While disdaining church as we've known it, Millennials embrace a gospel encompassing community, open communication, and intergenerational relationships. Microchurch is right up their alley. Think of all the times Jesus met with people over food, and you get the idea.

Reason 6: High-Functioning Ministry

Along with intimacy comes the opportunity for members to minister to each other. The subject of spiritual gifts (Romans 12, 1 Corinthians 12, and Ephesians 4) goes missing in many churches. A discussion around those passages would lead to a more in-depth experience of the Holy Spirit. Microchurches can do this in ways that a congregation numbering even just 50 persons cannot.

Today's more traditional churches are hierarchical, as are most megachurches. A few people control everything. A microchurch tends to operate around a circle where everybody plays. Close proximity and deep relationships call for and enfold more interaction with the Holy Spirit.

Reason 7: Expanded Reach

Most large American congregations are middle-class, heterosexual, and white or African American. Unnoticed homogeneity is a danger, and if it is intentional, it smacks of racism or willful exclusion of people for whom Jesus died.

We live among hundreds of immigrant groups who will never hear the gospel. As to sexuality, it is hard to believe that Jesus died for only heterosexual people. What about the homeless or substance abusers? Do you think God doesn't love the mega-wealthy who will not feel at home in your average middle-class church? Loving those overlooked by organized religion is a valid reason to plant a microchurch. After all, who will evangelize those who speak the 224 languages represented in Los Angeles County?[7]

Perhaps the easiest way for a congregation to multiply is to plant microchurches in a kind of hub-and-spoke process.

Leaders develop microchurches within the larger circle of a congregation then "graduate" to planting autonomous (or semi-autonomous) microchurches. The power in this is threefold: a) the size of the sending church is immaterial because of limited costs; b) planters develop naturally by planting from within before planting without; and c) the most significant benefit is the natural flow of "persons of peace" within a congregation reaching across cultural boundaries to plant microchurches within their particular people groups.

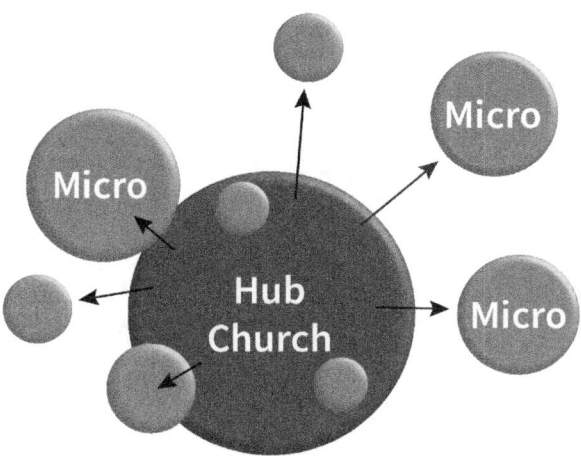

A hub church can launch microchurches within the congregation then move the more productive groups outside as autonomous churches. A faster approach is to identify individuals Jesus described as "persons of peace" with the hub supporting their efforts to disciple their unique people group.

Now we know what constitutes a microchurch and some reasons to start one. Let's look a little further at the qualifications for a leader and then at how to go about planting a microchurch.

CHAPTER 5

Who Should Start a Microchurch (or Several)?

Truth travels between people at the rate of trust—trust created by honest transparency, not perfection. This paradox means that leadership is not the practice of doing everything correctly but assessing circumstances and creating an environment where others can follow you into a better life, though they, and you, will stumble along your way.

Specialization and Spiritual Gifts

We live in a time of specialization. You can understand why the education of an oncologist differs from that of a cardiologist—or a plumber. However, the prevailing church model builds upon generalists, not specialists. The American Evangelical Church inherited a "priestly" model from Catholicism. One guy has all the responsibility and all the power.

Sure, big churches hire people to fill specialized roles, but most congregations still number fewer than a hundred people. As a result, we've pretty much ignored the Scriptural approach to specialization—spiritual gifts.

The Bible describes different God-driven abilities and ties them together under the leadership of the Spirit. It also describes Christ-followers as members of Christ's body, with each person contributing (1 Corinthians 12). Churches should not center on a single leader or a handful of them. The New Testament norm is that every person serves—some call this the "priesthood of every believer." We can only ever hope to achieve the priesthood of every believer if we embrace the specialization born of spiritual gifts and learn to remove the burden from a kingpin leader while spreading it among our membership.

You Can Do This

The Bible describes five primary categories of leaders: a) apostles—people who open new territory; b) prophets—those who keep us on the narrow path to life; c) evangelists—those particularly good at sharing faith; d) shepherds—leaders who bind us together; and e) teachers—those who love to study and share information. The Bible explains that each of these people is a gift to the Church. Their purpose is to *equip everyone* to serve others.

Using this logic, an evangelist brings people to know God and helps the rest of us in our efforts to introduce people to Christ. Evangelists utilize their gifts to equip the rest of us to participate in our part of the ministry.

If you chose to read this far, I assume that you have apostolic, evangelistic, or shepherding tendencies. You want to start something, and you hope to share it with others. There is no special training required for this task other than being discipled by someone who does it well. But you must discover your particular mix of leadership gifts then begin stimulating the gifts you spot in others.

Microchurch Success

I have a friend in Sri Lanka who launched a movement of more than 2,000 churches in that war-torn country beginning in 1983. Most are microchurches led by people who don't earn a living from them. I call these people "bivocational, single-salary microchurch pastors."

They maintain secular employment from intent, not as a fallback. Sure, some churches have grown to the point that a pastor must quit their day job, but this group would rather multiply small churches than add people to build a big one. They understand that multiplication trumps addition if you want to change a culture.

On my first trip to Sri Lanka, I met a wealthy man who imports all the BMWs that enter the country. But what lights his fire is that he pastors two microchurches (at 4 p.m. and 7 p.m. each Sunday) while attending his home church on Sunday mornings. The night we met, he had said goodbye to his 7 p.m. congregation and was off to start another the following week. He has no formal training other than what he got from his mentor. (He is a "trivocational," single-salary microchurch pastor and planter.)

These people rapidly spread the gospel in a nation that is 74% Buddhist. Some Americans use the term *co-vocational* to describe leaders who are passionate about both their ministry work and their secular job. I like the term but wonder whether ordinary people might have difficulty understanding the inevitable abbreviation, "covo." I prefer the term *freelance pastor*.

Vocabulary is essential because it often shapes behavior. Both words describe a person who maintains a job or career that pays the bills while leading a church without a salary. Choose whichever works for you, but I'll go with the one that seems more adaptable to the larger culture.

Bivocational or Freelance as Normal

We often hear the Apostle Paul described as a tentmaker. That appears to have been a *fallback* for when he lacked funds to travel and establish new churches.

Scripture paints a different picture of his employers, Aquila and Priscilla, and their ministry. They were tentmakers who planted a ministry in Corinth before Paul arrived (Acts 18:1-3). They did more of the same in Ephesus (Acts 18:18-26) and Rome (Romans 16:3). Aquila and Priscilla seem to have embraced it as their primary funding source, even after engaging in ministry. They planted from their career.

Bivocational pastorates are becoming more prevalent. Most of the microchurch leaders I've met hold successful careers. This approach may be necessary for church planters in an era where many churches seem to scramble to grow just to make budget.

A new appreciation for bivocational ministry would also liberate the Church to infiltrate the culture. We should understand that every children's church worker and home group leader is a single-salary bivocational pastor. What about Christ-followers leading Bible studies in their offices or mentoring people in a homeless shelter? Or the architect in my church who disciples young men out of poverty toward a meaningful career? Each of these is a bivocational pastor. So is the person leading a microchurch! A lot more microchurches led by bivocational pastors could reverse the slide of American Christianity from oblivion to meaningful contribution to society.

Most Millennials don't want to become full-time pastors but would rather keep their professions and use the marketplace as a platform for ministry. We should support this tendency instead of trying to force young people into an increasingly obsolete model.

More than 70% of the populace vote with their feet, proving that they are not interested in whatever the church's prevailing model does to attract members.

The church of the near future will not support the economic overhang of congregations in the recent past. We will rely on pastors and church planters who can "make tents" while making disciples. If the sentence you just read describes you, I wrote this book with you in mind. You represent our future, and I think you represent it well.

Learning from History

In the 17th and 18th centuries, Methodists on the American frontier trained young pastors in the homes of veteran pastors in between trips among a circuit of churches. Fledgling pastors spent "saddle time" reading books from the mentor's library. A circuit might include dozens of small meetings effectively led by a member of the community. Entry to ministry required college graduation.

Baptists lowered the bar. They required no formal education and trained future church planters in a local congregation. These folks were often accused of handing a new convert a Bible and sending him off to plant a church in the frontier. I hope you'll notice that there are more Baptist churches in America than any other.

In their book *The Wholehearted Church Planter*, Linda Bergquist and Allan Karr describe the criteria for planting a church as someone knowing and loving God while knowing and loving people. I would add to that formula a simple passion for making disciples. Let's look at some modern-day examples.

Learning from Others

Most of us learn by observation, so I want to conclude this chapter with a few stories for you to ponder. Each person described below comes at microchurch from a different angle, with differing goals and quite different results. Yet each is successful in his or her own way. I hope their stories bless you nearly as much as their friendships bless me.

Ryan Delameter: OCNWTR Churches

Ryan leads a growing microchurch network from a coffee shop in San Clemente, California.

After suffering a painful divorce, he decided to clear his head with a long bicycle ride—a very long ride. He rode from Southern California to British Columbia, then across Canada to Nova Scotia and back to California. Ryan hopped on the bike, not yet satisfied, pedaling to Columbia, South America.

As a surfer, he naturally explored beach towns along the way, where he discovered people who were getting sick from the brackish water they drank. That birthed an idea. He would come home and plant a church that supplied clean drinking water to impoverished Latin American beach towns.

The next moves were in tandem. He landed a job at Saddleback Church as a youth pastor while earning a doctorate in environmental science.

Ryan left Saddleback and planted a microchurch in a mixed martial arts studio in San Clemente. The church soon built an ocean water desalinization plant while planting another church in El Salvador. The MMA church moved to a coffee shop when it launched Taco Tuesdays, complete with worship music and a short Bible teaching.

Once the group discovered that there were 35,000-plus non-franchised coffee shops across America, they saw the potential for a microchurch movement. These businesses operate from morning until around 5:30 p.m., leaving evenings open for other possibilities. No pastor is paid. The microchurches meet on weeknights while paying little or no rent.

As I write, the network has planted microchurches in five wealthy Southern California beach towns, El Salvador, and Buenos Aires (where the pastor is an American who plays professional basketball in that country). Aside from El Salvador, the new churches thrive in cities where planting a prevailing-model, big-budget church is prohibitively expensive. COVID-19 slowed the movement overseas, but when the pandemic dies down, the group has government permission to plant desalinization microchurches in Indonesia and Bangladesh, both Muslim countries. The more than 35,000 independent coffee shops give them nearly unlimited potential to multiply in the United States.

Randall Ishida: People with a "Past"

A half-dozen years ago, Randy stumbled into a congregation I led after feeling stifled in a prevailing-model church. It seems that Randy exercising his gifts threatened the kingpin pastor.

Randy had been discipling a man he met while working out in a local gym. The man and his wife were planning to commit suicide when he met Randy and began following him as he followed Jesus.

I encouraged Randy to expand his disciplemaking into a microchurch with this man's friends. Randy is a retired police officer who felt enough compassion for people he had locked away to assist them in job hunts, etc., when they exited prison. The combination was a natural fit, and there were soon two microchurches focused on people coming out of jail in Honolulu.

Randy eventually accompanied me to St. Petersburg, Russia, where I taught a microchurch-planting seminar to local pastors. Before the week was up, Randy began coaching a middle-aged Russian who had recently connected with Jewish people from Turkey. Growing up in a Muslim context, they wanted to learn about Jesus, or *Issa*. Randy continued coaching his new friend via Zoom and Facebook after returning home. That man eventually moved to Crimea, where he started several microchurches in small towns while operating his business as a personal trainer.

Fast-forward to today. Four months ago, doctors informed Randy that his body was riddled with cancer, giving him just five weeks to live. His immediate reaction was to get busy hastening his apprentices to take charge of the microchurches he currently leads in Oahu (he'd already handed off the earlier micro-plants). The current crew is men struggling with addictions and living in halfway houses.

The Lord stretched Randy's time on this earth through experimental medications. He still works his job, leads two microchurches, and mentors disciples to take his slot when he "moves away."

Parker Green: Launching as a Microchurch Network

Parker Green planted a microchurch in Huntington Beach, California, intending to launch a church multiplication movement.

He grew up in ministry. Bob and Mavis Green, Parker's parents, were early members of the first Hope Chapel and have led congregations ever since. Parker served in youth ministry at Hillsong in Australia alongside his brother-in-law, Paul Andrew. Parker joined the team when Paul planted Liberty Church in New York City. Leaving there, he headed across the country to launch a microchurch multiplication movement.

The last time we spoke, there were eight Salt Churches. A freelance planter leads each. They gather monthly as one large group. They plan to reduce the monthly meetings to once each quarter. That may be advantageous, as it would permit the leaders of churches they've planted in other cities to attend. Though still a fledgling movement, they are already growing in "hub cities" across the country.

When I last talked to Parker, he told me that all this costs next to nothing. Groups meet in homes, backyards, parks, and coffee shops. Nobody gets a salary. Rent is negligible or free. There is no government involvement and no tax receipts, as they encourage members to give their tithes to people in need and do so in Jesus' name.

Keiko Uyeda: Japanese Wives Living in Honolulu

Japanese people must love Hawaii. One-fourth of the population in the state are Japanese Americans. All this results in many businesses operating back and forth across the Pacific.

Women hold careers in Japan, but if a husband gets a job that takes the family to Hawaii, his wife usually finds it difficult to obtain a work visa from our government. Couple that with the fact that most Japanese women with children at home choose not to work, and you have many women looking for friendship with others from their home country.

Keiko Uyeda is a divorcee who chose to stay in America after her husband's misadventures. A highly successful businesswoman, she is also a strong disciplemaker. One of my closest friends planted and leads a large church-multiplying congregation in Osaka, Japan. It was Keiko who discipled him toward ministry many years ago.

Today she leads a Japanese-language microchurch for Japanese women living in Hawaii. Her success is a signpost pointing the rest of us to unreached people groups living all around us. In my neighborhood, they may be Syrians or serious skateboarders. Whatever the case, Jesus told us to disciple the "people groups." Many such groups will never enter a church or hear the gospel unless we take it to them, much like Keiko is taking the Church to people living in America but not speaking our language.

John Harris: Online Microchurch Growing Beyond Expectation

John Harris was a career military chaplain. After retiring, he spent a dozen years as an executive pastor in a large California church. Then he resigned to launch a consulting business.

That was great for a couple of months; until COVID-19 hit.

John quickly took his business online. But then the fun began. Mostly coaching pastors, he met a wall of resistance over the idea of doing church via the internet. His clientele was bent on returning to church as it was in 2019.

Already mining the possibilities extant in online communications, John worked hard to get a bunch of pastors to appreciate the new tools. That didn't work so well, which led John to realize that he needed to demonstrate rather than lecture others about online church.

John planted a microchurch on Facebook. He posted an announcement, and a tiny church was born. John would teach through a livestream on Wednesday evenings then join the members via the comment tool on the platform. As it grew to 400 people in eight months, the group began dividing people into "in-house online microchurches" using the "rooms" feature of Facebook. They even planted two face-to-face microchurches that grew out of the Facebook congregation.

As micro grew into macro, the fellowship quotient diminished. The answer was to combine Facebook with Zoom for a more personalized experience.

John has no intention of renting a building and confining their church to a geographic location. Membership is too widespread for that. John asks the question, "What would have happened to the Church if COVID-19 had hit before God gave us social media and tools like Zoom?" His is just one more example of what God can do if we are smart enough to let the Spirit lead us into new territory.

CHAPTER 6

How to Start a Microchurch

The Scripture says, "Trust in the Lord with all your heart, and lean not on your own understanding; In all your ways acknowledge Him, and He shall direct your paths" (Proverbs 3:5-6 NKJV).

In other words, you don't need formal training, but you do need to hear from God—not just about starting a microchurch but about life itself.

I can remember being called (in a weird vision) to plant a church in Hawaii. My friend Aaron Suzuki and I, along with our wives, Ruby and Stephanie, prayed on it for five years before relocating. I'm not saying to pray for five years before starting a microchurch (unless you're moving 2,500 miles) but do seek the mind of God.

Know Your Calling

If you want to start a microchurch, you must have a specific group of people in mind.

Of course, if you already know some people who need a new church, everything is pretty set for you. However, if you expect to expand the Kingdom of God into unchartered territory, you will need to ask the Lord about who you should reach. You may feel called to a specific location without knowing the people groups who need to know Jesus in that place. Starting without partners is a little more challenging than starting with existing relationships, but it is certainly doable. The key will be asking God for connections into whichever slice of the sociological pie he assigns to you.

My wife and I "parachuted" into Manhattan Beach, California, to plant our first church. We landed there without knowing a soul in the community. For years I felt a calling to that specific location without knowing much about the place or the people who lived there. I'd had a couple of supernatural encounters pointing us to the area before doors suddenly opened for us to move from the San Fernando Valley to an empty building in this SoCal beach town.

But spiritual direction aside, we felt lost when faced with a new community and knowing no one there. Our answer was to recruit a half dozen friends from nearby communities. One girl brought her friend on our second Sunday—later that week, another friend and I introduced this new girl to Jesus. She proved to be an evangelist. She immediately told others about Jesus. A couple of weeks later, my wife and I found ourselves living in a middle-class community but pastoring a bunch of hippies and a few bikers. We discovered our unique calling almost by accident.

You may be uniquely plugged into a microcosm of society. Maybe your relatives are recent immigrants. Perhaps you are a policeman. Maybe you're a wealthy person. Perhaps you live in a "housing project." Who are your Facebook friends? Ask yourself what distinguishes you from the general populace. The answer will point to the kind of people you should expect to disciple into a relationship with God. These people constitute your circle of influence. They should define the microchurch you plant.

Have a Plan

I recently retired from full-time pastoring after doing it for a very long time. Back in 1971, I planted a microchurch, but it didn't remain micro for long. I was not bivocational, though I might have claimed to be a freelancer since we planted the church while relying on our savings as our sole means of support. When I retired, I left Hawaii after 35 years and two pastorates and moved to San Diego, where I hoped to plant a microchurch in the LGBTQ community. That didn't work out.

I currently work part-time for Exponential.org and also train pastors internationally. COVID-19 interrupted our relationship with a church we had helped get off the ground in San Diego, but my wife and I now lead two microchurches via Zoom. We've found deep intimacy in both groups. There is something about the buffer of the computer screen that allows people to be even more open with each other than they would be if we met face-to-face.

My point? I've only ever led two stand-alone microchurches, though I've led dozens of microchurches within larger congregations. I've directly coached around 80 church planters, with the resulting outfall numbering around 2,400 churches worldwide. In other words, I know a lot about planting mid-size churches and much about microchurches within a larger congregation, and I believe that translates into enough experience that whatever I hope to add to your toolkit is valid.

Also, I wrote a book called *Mega Multi Micro* for Exponential. (You can find it at Exponential.org.) It addresses why megachurches have not done all we expected and why we need to multiply microchurches that might grow to whatever size the Spirit has in mind. The book and ensuing seminars put me in touch with many microchurch planters. Every one of them maintains a full-time job or career. These are freelance pastors. It's their wisdom, along with my experience, that I'm trying to include in these pages.

Wow—glad to get that off my chest! Now I feel ready to lay out some strategies.

Strategy

The following few paragraphs are *not* strategies for you or your microchurch to duplicate. They are *thought starters* to help you get moving.

There are several elements that you must cover if you want to multiply disciples who could multiply microchurches. So, here are strategic elements to a microchurch that I believe are universally applicable. You may want to fit all the following onto small cards, so your members can share the material with friends.

Our Purpose

Recently, a pastor I'm coaching sent me two single-spaced, typed pages delineating a value statement for a church he hopes to plant. I asked him to simplify and sloganize that content to: a) fit on a half-page double-spaced; and b) express their values in easy-to-remember slogans.

The churches I led sloganized Jesus' two greatest commandments with this simple statement, "We promise to love you . . . as is!"

You'll quickly notice that the slogan doesn't mention God, but everyone in those churches knows that we're to love God and love our neighbor because we happen to say that every week (along with the third-greatest command—the Great Commission).

Offer
- God but not religion.
- Scripture but no sermons, ever! (Everyone is a learner/teacher.)
- A focus on people, not behaviors.
- A welcome to everyone, even if they hate God.

Operate
- With potluck food and fellowship (beer, Bible, and barbeque?).
- Using open discussions around pre-arranged Scriptures.
- Without an offering. (But we will press you to help your neighbors or give to a mission.) This works well in a home, coffee shop, or even a bar but would change if rented real estate, etc., becomes necessary.
- With a desire to duplicate whatever we discover.
- Knowing that successive leaders will come only from within our ranks.

Expect to Multiply

It's probably best to start small unless you are trying to unite a group of church refugees.

You'll find pushback against rapid reproduction or multiplication of congregations if you fall into the "transfer trap." Believers bored with other churches paradoxically end up trying to duplicate whatever they left behind, though they found it distasteful. Building a church through relational disciplemaking is slow to start but yields exponential growth.

Beginning with a handful of serious people is best. The goal is to make disciples rather than making "Christians." The word *Christian* carries a lot of baggage. Jesus said to make disciples; he didn't tell us to make converts and *then* disciple them. If you can connect with unchurched people and let them discover spiritual pathways through Scriptural discussions with each other, you will see success. In other words, don't preach! Instead, let your people discover fresh insights as they mutually examine biblical truths.

Train New Leaders

As the group grows, disciple "apprentice leaders" who could run the existing group while you go about launching a new one. Leaving the current group in the hands of the apprentice gives that person the benefit of leading an established group in a familiar meeting place. It helps ensure the group's success while delivering to you, the more experienced leader, the refreshment and renewal that comes with pioneering a new group. (By the way, starting in your home blocks you from leaving the group to plant another. So avoid this if you can.)

Prefer Multiplication over Addition

People learn best through interaction, and everyone craves intimacy.

Choose to multiply churches rather than grow a big one. From my experience, if you grow past a dozen people meeting in a home, you need to meet in two or three rooms after a shared meal. Microchurches in bars and coffee shops top out at seven to nine people before multiplying. God may cause your microchurch to go macro—that's his business. But for your part, plan to multiply instead of adding. You'll be glad you did.

CHAPTER 7

A Template to Modify (Plus a Few Tips)

I'm hesitant to write the following few paragraphs because every group is different, and each has its own needs and personality. I only offer these ideas as suggestions. You can modify them to fit your unique circumstances, gifting, and the needs of those you encounter.

Eat Together
People make friends over food.

I like to spend the first half-hour of our time together over food. I love leftovers because they bring a story with them! Eating coupled with fellowship allows latecomers to arrive in time for the Bible discussion. The best part of this time is the bonding that takes place. And, when God answers a prayer, everyone gets to hear about it.

Keep It Relational
I know I've already said this, but you must avoid the temptation to preach. It is far better to let the Bible speak for itself. I like to either hand out photocopies of Scripture passages (whole chapters of the Bible) or assign a chapter to read ahead of time if everyone owns a Bible.

The ground rules are these: a) if you read the Scripture five times during the week, you can talk from the beginning of the meeting; b) if you didn't read, you should keep quiet for the first 20 minutes. Those rules accomplish two things. First, everyone is motivated to read and meditate on Scripture. Second, a person who didn't read won't disrupt the discussion by heading down some detour. He or she will know where everyone else is headed before jumping in.

Ask Important Questions
Asking questions like these helps people move beyond an intellectual exercise into anticipation of interaction with God. Questions along these lines are helpful:
- What did you find fascinating about the passage we read?
- Did it frustrate you? Why?
- What do you think God is saying to humanity through these words?
- Is he saying anything to you personally?
- If he is, what will you do about it within the next 48 hours? How can the rest of us help?
- Is there another person who should hear what you've just told us?

Where and When to Meet
It's nice to meet in homes because of the freedom you find there. You can even break out a guitar and sing if you like. But in an urban environment, parking issues, etc., may make this impractical.

Restaurants, coffee shops, and conference rooms work well, though they restrict freedom. Parks and outdoor spaces are ideal in nice weather, though I know of two churches that met in snowy parks for months—one in Tokyo and the other in Kyiv, Ukraine. In some cultures, people resist meeting in homes. For these people, a public space may be most desirable.

Don't fall for the "once-a-month for busy people" argument. If you meet weekly and someone goes on a business trip, that person misses their friends for only 13 days. If you meet bi-weekly, that turns into 27 days. Once a month? I think you get the picture.

It's also a good idea to meet for smaller one-on-one lunches or coffee with another group member. Close-up meetings become more crucial as you become familiar with each other and become a support team through life's ups and downs. Let's take a clue from the early Church, who Scripture depicts as meeting daily.

Doctrine and Other Heavy-Sounding Words

Somebody got worked up because I placed this material after the "how-to" stuff in this book. To that person, doctrine comes first. But there is a problem with Bible doctrines—we too often utilize them as filters, improper filters.

Ecclesiology (the doctrine depicting Church life and practice) divides Christ-followers more than any other issue. The Greek word for *church* is *ecclesia*, meaning "called-out ones." Originally used to describe city officials, Jesus used it to describe a people called out to bless the general population.

The concept of a group of people called to change the world for the better is simultaneously complex and straightforward. It could describe a couple of people doing something for another, or it could serve to mean an entire denomination. We need a working definition.

A Minimal Ecclesiology

We were at dinner when a well-meaning friend challenged me to defend my ecclesiology because it allowed for microchurches. It seems his hang-up was over a church too small to boast an "elder board." But, before I could respond by asking where he found elder boards in the New Testament, another friend interrupted, "Ralph, don't answer him until he can defend his ecclesiology, which allows for all the nonbiblical functions in the megachurch he leads."

Need I tell you that neither of us defined our ecclesiology after that? The megachurch pastor swallowed the fact that much of what we see as standard in the American church is not biblical—not necessarily wrong, but not biblical at the root. And there are missing elements in that model, such as shared meals, deep fellowship, and fully activated spiritual gifts.

When describing ecclesial minimums, a misconception can arise suggesting that we're trying to get away with something—kind of like cheating on a term paper in high school by copying from Wikipedia.

Don't Put the Cart Before the Horse

The real problem with any ecclesiology is putting the cart before the horse. My friend Brian Sanders suggests we need to address doctrinal positions in this order: Christology, Missiology, Ecclesiology.

Your life must be rooted first in Christ, then in his mission. Emerging from the example of Jesus, coupled with the mission, will fall a working doctrine of the Church. And it will fit the circumstances in which you live and operate, be it Utah or Uganda. Confuse the order of your "ologies," and you get into trouble.

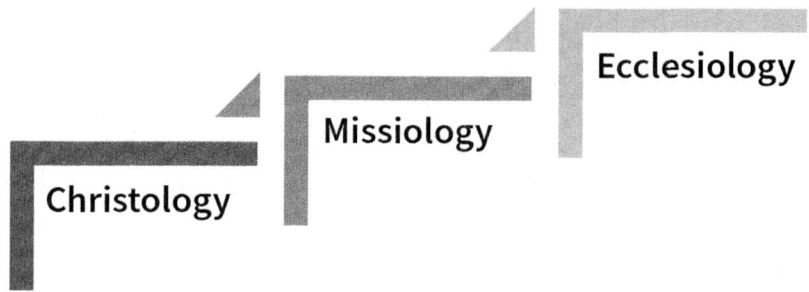

It is crucial that you understand how each of these systems of thought, or Bible doctrines, build upon Jesus as our foundation. To begin church strategies from a doctrine of the Church confuses both the gospel and our mission. Learn to think in this order—Jesus, his/our mission, and finally, whatever church form emerges.

Put the mission first, and you can call anything church. You must start with Jesus and his disciplemaking example, move to live the Great Commission, and then discover church.

That's precisely what happened to the earliest Christ-followers. Put your ecclesiology first, and it becomes a sorting tool rejecting anything that doesn't reflect your personal, sometimes mistaken, beliefs. Think about this: most people's understanding of the Church comes through what worked for other people in another place at another time. It is rooted in the opinions of men rather than the actual living out of the Great Commission.

Keep It Orderly

God is a God of order, so you need to maintain a level of control that is consistent with your theology. For some, even lifting hands in worship doesn't work. Others have more freedom of expression. But you should remember Paul's words, "God is not a God of confusion but of peace" (1 Corinthians 14:33 ESV). And again, "All things should be done decently and in order" (1 Corinthians 14:40 ESV).

The broader context of those two passages includes chapters 12-14 of 1 Corinthians. Paul speaks primarily to the use of spiritual gifts in the Church. Chapter 13 tells that love is more important than miracles, but put together, all three endorse the miraculous—but in an orderly fashion.

Make Disciples, Not Churches

Don't forget that this is still about making disciples.

Jesus told his disciple Peter, "I will build my church, and all the powers of hell will not conquer it" (Matthew 16:18 NLT). He later told Peter that his job (and ours) is to tend his sheep and feed them. This is a pastor's role. It all falls under the category of disciplemaking rather than church building.

When disciplemaking is fully operational, then organizing churches becomes necessary. That happened in Acts 11, when persecuted Christ-followers (who we first met in Acts 8) took the good news of God's love to other cities. We read more along these lines in Acts 14, when Paul sneaked into towns he'd previously visited and appointed elders (pastors) from among the disciples he had made earlier.

The bigger New Testament picture is church planting following disciplemaking, rather than the other way around. Effective disciplemaking brings new people into the circle of God's love. As the family grows, organizing people into groups naturally follows—disciples making disciples forces either church growth (addition) or church multiplication.

Today we spend money on marketing, gather a core of primarily believers from existing churches, and then stage a huge "launch day" that attracts more Christ-followers from surrounding congregations. Many of these people come because they were disgruntled where they were. After that, we're surprised at the low commitment level among our members.

Make disciples among non-believers first, then start a microchurch. It's far more straightforward, less expensive, and more effective. If God wants it to become macro, that's up to him, and there will be little you could do to stop him. Jesus builds the Church; we disciple people into his kingdom and feed his sheep.

Microchurch Tensions You Will Encounter

Life is not without its problems. You are bound to face several tensions if you decide to plant a microchurch. We'll look at a few of them here. Being forewarned means being forearmed.

People Who Flake Out

My biggest frustration as a church planter comes from believing in people, giving them my precious time, and then being disappointed by them. Some folks resist any movement forward in their relationship with God. For others, it is an unwillingness to commit time and energy to minister to others. Some just abandon you for whatever is new in town. Jesus predicted this in the parable of the four soils. It's going to happen, so get used to it.

Addition and Multiplication

If things go as well as you hope they do, you will be tempted to move from micro to macro.

There is the lure of pastoral ministry for some as a full-time job. An inability to delegate may exacerbate the pressure to go full-time—you find yourself doing more than you should, so you choose to get paid rather than spread the opportunities.

There is also the issue of ego.

A crowd can boost your morale but make you miss the bigger picture of Christ's kingdom on earth. We'll always reach more people in more unreached clusters if we choose to multiply churches rather than try to get big at any cost. Of course, God may be calling you to grow beyond a microchurch. No problem! Just be sure you start a bunch of others along the way.

Also be aware that, as you grow, the dynamics of a group will change. A self-discovery microchurch morphs into a different animal as it expands beyond a dozen people. Discussions center on the thoughts of only a few people, limiting participation and self-learning. Grow past 30, and you'll end up preparing sermons. There is nothing wrong with either option, but you should anticipate the tension before facing it.

Controllers

Most new churches attract a few people who want to control but not lead. I've faced these people in all three of the larger churches I planted. Usually, they are attention seekers who won't lay down their lives for others. If they *were* willing, they'd be doing what you do. It is the disease of people who want to be big fish in small ponds!

Sometimes former pastors or even seminary graduates who never "made the cut" will invade your group. These people have a call from God in their lives but have never found a way to fulfill it. They try to solve their issues by manipulating you.

Beware of anyone insisting on a position in your flock during the first few weeks. Also, don't fall for the newcomer's handshake with the $50 bill in it—that's a sure sign of someone trying to gain the upper hand.

Doctrine Fighters

Just Google anything from "the return of Christ" to "speaking in tongues" to "women in ministry" or "homosexuality," and you'll find dozens of self-appointed experts who lead nothing but a website. Or Google the name of any prominent pastor you know, and you'll find a whole raft of trash-talkers tearing at another person's reputation. Toss in Donald Trump, Hillary Clinton, or Bernie Sanders, and you'll discover another bunch of amateur theologians.

My point here is that you can't allow people like this to take over your meetings. You may even agree with whatever they say, but a church is not the place to divide people via arguments. People come for refuge—provide it. A simple statement of purpose and an equally simple doctrine statement can help ward off argumentative people.

Professional Criticism

Start a microchurch, and other Christians will question your motives. "It's not a real church." "What gives you the right to do this?" "Are you in competition with the church you came from?" Another form of this is the criticism from leaders who worry about losing members (translate that: money) to a new movement.

All these and more await you. Just be calm. Stay loving and patiently ignore your critics.

Your Task

We often make it our job to multiply "Christians" rather than committed disciplemakers. And even church planting can become a rabbit hole. So here is a reminder of your job description:

> We have stopped evaluating others from a human point of view.
> At one time we thought of Christ merely from a human point of

view. How differently we know him now! This means that anyone who belongs to Christ has become a new person. The old life is gone; a new life has begun!

All of this is a gift from God, who brought us back to himself through Christ. And God has given us this task of reconciling people to him. For God was in Christ, reconciling the world to himself, no longer counting people's sins against them. And he gave us this wonderful message of reconciliation. So we are Christ's ambassadors; God is making his appeal through us. We speak for Christ when we plead, "Come back to God!" For God made Christ, who never sinned, to be the offering for our sin, so that we could be made right with God through Christ (2 Corinthians 5:16-21 NLT).

Jesus calls us to make disciples who obey him to the point of making more disciples. The directive in Matthew begins with Jesus reminding us that he has all authority—he is God. Disciplemaking is the pathway to reconciling people to their creator. This action is about him, not us or our organizations.

Christian, your role is about expanding the Kingdom of God to people who need it. There is no better calling than this!

APPENDIX A

Questions to Loosen Up a New Group

I've found it helpful to ask non-threatening questions to help a group of relative strangers bond. The questions may seem nerdy, but I guarantee that they will make your people feel more comfortable with each other.

Try these the first week:
1. Who are you, and how did you get involved with the rest of us?
2. What is your favorite flavor of ice cream?
3. Can you name your favorite song from your high school years? Why did you like it?
4. How did your family heat (or cool) your home when you were five years old?

The second week:
5. If you could change anything about the world, what would that be?
6. If you could sit in a room with God, what would you ask him?

These questions will help put everyone at ease. They also get people in the mode of self-revelation, which becomes essential as you discuss Scripture and encourage each other in your walk with God.

ABOUT THE AUTHOR

Ralph Moore is the founding pastor of three churches that grew into the Hope Chapel movement, now numbering more than 2,300 churches worldwide. These are the offspring of the 70+ congregations launched from Ralph's hands-on disciplemaking efforts.

He currently serves as "church multiplication catalyzer" for Exponential. In addition to this, he travels the globe, teaching church multiplication to pastors in startup movements. He has authored several books, including *Making Disciples*, *How to Multiply Your Church*, *Starting a New Church*, *Defeating Anxiety*, and *Let Go of the Ring: The Hope Chapel Story*. Check out his blog at www.RalphMoore.net

APPENDIX B

Suggested Scriptures for Discussion

Here is a list of Scriptures that you might assign for discussion. Microchurches are built around self-discovery through the Scriptures, with the Holy Spirit as our guide. No preaching necessary.

Print out each passage in two translations—one being a literal translation (word by word), such as the English Standard Version of the Bible (ESV), and the other a conceptual translation (thought by thought), such as the New Living Translation (NLT).

Ask each person to read the passage at least five times during the week, writing short notes to themselves as they do. Meditating on Scripture changes lives (Psalm 1). Only allow those who have read the material to speak during the first 20 minutes when you meet. Others can join after the readers set the tone of the discussion. Each passage below should be good for one week.

1. Psalm 1—Blessings and choices
2. Romans 12:1-2—Commitment to God
3. John 3:1-21 and Numbers 21:8-9—Trust in God (Note: Cereuses, the symbol for medicine, comes from this Numbers passage.)
4. 1 John 1:8–2:2—Forgiveness
5. 1 Corinthians 13—Love for others
6. Matthew 22:36-40—Loving God and others
7. Matthew 6:1-4—Doing good out of love
8. Hebrews 10:23-25—Stimulating each other to love and good deeds
9. 1 John 4:7-21—Hate toward others
10. Matthew 6:5-15—How to pray
11. John 15:1-17—Sticking close to Jesus, answered prayer

After you exhaust the list (or before that), you can read through entire books of the Bible thought by thought rather than chapter by chapter. One option is Discovery Bible Study as a central focus for meetings with a more dynamic approach. Another is to use the YouVersion app in conjunction with Bible Project videos.

A NOTE FROM RALPH

Thank you for reading this book. If you know another leader who might benefit from this book, please pass it along.

I invite you to visit my website: www.RalphMoore.net.

You might also enjoy the 18-minute video, "Microchurch: What Is It and How Do You Justify It?" at https://youtu.be/8dOexzNa0jE.

ENDNOTES

Chapter 3

1. Kelly Shattuck, "7 Startling Facts: A Close Look at Church Attendance in America," *Church Leaders*, December 29, 2015, https://churchleaders.com/pastors/pastor-articles/139575-7-startling-facts-an-up-close-look-at-church-attendance-in-america.html.

2. Wilhelm Bacher and Lewis N. Dembitz, "Synagogue," *JewishEncyclopedia.com*, http://www.jewishencyclopedia.com/articles/14160-synagogue.

Chapter 4

3. Ed Stetzer, "Nominals to Nones: 3 Key Takeaways from Pew's Religious Landscape Survey," *Christianity Today*, May 2015.

4. David T. Olson and Craig Groeschel, The American Church in Crisis (Grand Rapids, MI: Zondervan, 2008), 120.

5. David Barrett and Todd Johnson, *World Christian Trends* (Pasadena: William Carey Library, 2001), 841.

6. Ed Stetzer, "Can Small Be Healthy?" *Facts & Trends*, March 30, 2016.

7. "Top Languages Spoken in Los Angeles," Geos Languages Plus, LA, https://www.geosla.net/jp/misc/daily_student_life/languages_spoken_in_los_angeles.htm.

ABOUT THE AUTHOR

Ralph Moore is the founding pastor of three churches that grew into the Hope Chapel movement, now numbering more than 2,300 churches worldwide. These are the offspring of the 70+ congregations launched from Ralph's hands-on disciplemaking efforts.

He currently serves as "church multiplication catalyzer" for Exponential. In addition to this, he travels the globe, teaching church multiplication to pastors in startup movements. He has authored several books, including *Making Disciples, How to Multiply Your Church, Starting a New Church, Defeating Anxiety,* and *Let Go of the Ring: The Hope Chapel Story.* Check out his blog at www.RalphMoore.net.

Printed in Great Britain
by Amazon